Manners

Manners in the Classroom

by Terri DeGezelle

Consultant:
Madonna Murphy, PhD, Professor of Ed
University of St. Francis, Joliet, Illinois
Author, *Character Education in America's Blue Ribbo*

Capstone
press

Mankato, Minnesota

First Facts is published by Capstone Press
151 Good Counsel Drive, P.O. Box 669, Mankato, Minnesota 56002
www.capstonepress.com

Library of Congress Cataloging-in-Publication Data
DeGezelle, Terri, 1955–
    Manners in the classroom / by Terri DeGezelle.
    p. cm.—(First facts. Manners)
    Includes bibliographical references and index.
    ISBN 0-7368-2646-4 (hardcover)
    1. Etiquette for ▓▓▓▓▓▓▓ teenagers. 2. Children—Conduct of life. [1. Etiquette. 2. Schools.]
I. Title. ▓▓▓▓
BJ1857▓
395.1▓   2003024185

Su▓▓▓▓▓▓▓▓▓▓▓▓▓▓ and shows how different character values can be used in
▓▓▓▓▓▓▓▓▓▓▓▓▓▓▓▓

Cr▓▓▓▓▓▓▓▓▓▓▓▓▓▓Peters, designer; Wanda Winch, photo researcher; Eric Kudalis,
▓▓▓▓▓▓▓▓▓▓

Ph▓▓▓▓
All photographs by Capstone Press/Gem Photo Studio/Dan Delaney, except page 20,
    Photodisc Inc./David Buffington

Artistic Effects
Capstone Press/Juliette Peters, 21

1 2 3 4 5 6 09 08 07 06 05 04

Table of Contents

Time for School

The bell rings. It is time for school. Students use good **manners** as they get ready for school. People with good manners are kind and treat others with **respect**. Good manners help everyone learn and have fun in the classroom.

Fun Fact!
In the United States, about 53 million kids go to grade schools and high schools.

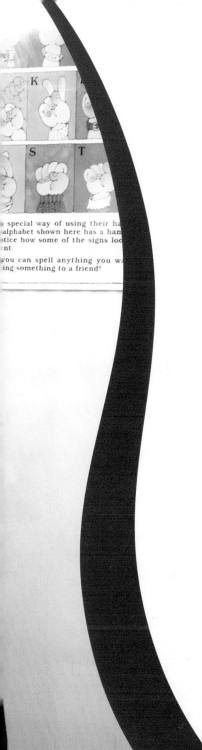

a special way of using their ha
alphabet shown here has a han
tice how some of the signs loo
nt.

you can spell anything you w
ing something to a friend!

Being Polite

Polite people treat others nicely. At school, polite kids say "good morning" to their teachers. They are on time for school. Polite students say "please" and "thank you" when they ask to **borrow** pencils or paper.

Fun Fact!
National Teacher Day honors U.S. teachers each year in May.

Being Patient

The teacher explains a project to the class. She gives directions. **Patient** kids listen to the teacher without **interrupting**.

Students raise their hands when they want to ask questions. Patient students wait for the teacher to call their names. Students then ask their questions.

Showing Respect

Students can respect others in the classroom. Respect is when people care about the thoughts and feelings of others. Kids show respect when they work quietly at their desks. They do not bother other students.

Being a Leader

Class leaders set good examples for others to follow. Some leaders help the teacher. They hand out paper and other supplies to students.

Some leaders help other students.
They help students with homework.
One student leads the line for lunch.
Leaders help everyone work together.

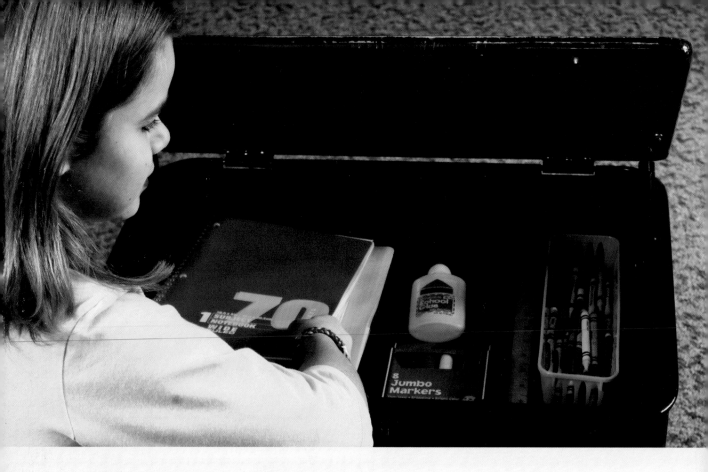

Keeping Neat

Students use good manners when they keep their classroom neat. They keep their desks clean. They **organize** their school supplies.

Students help each other keep the classroom neat. They pick up paper after art class. Students put away books and supplies.

Learning
Games

Choose one to begin

• Math
• Spelling
• Geography
• Biology

Being Kind

Kind people care about others. Kids can be kind at school in many ways. They can invite a friend to play a computer game. They can try to cheer up a friend who is feeling sad.

Good Manners

Good manners are important at school. Kids with good manners listen to directions. They help each other with class projects. They are kind to others. Good manners help everyone have a good day at school.

Fun Fact!
At least 6 million teachers work in classrooms at U.S. schools.

Amazing but True!

In the United States, at least 2 billion pencils are used each year. Each pencil can be used to write 45,000 words. The average pencil can draw a line 35 miles (56 kilometers) long.

Hands On: Kindness Box

Kind people show others they care. Let your classmates know that manners are important by making a kindness box. You can also make a kindness box to use with family members at home.

What You Need

shoe box
paint or markers
pieces of paper
pencils

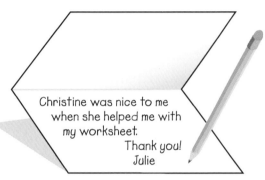

Christine was nice to me when she helped me with my worksheet.
Thank you!
Julie

What You Do

1. Decorate a shoe box with paint or markers.
2. Put pieces of paper and pencils by the box.
3. Ask your classmates to look for ways that people are kind to others at school.
4. Classmates should write down how someone was kind to others and put the paper in the kindness box.
5. At the end of each week, have your teacher read papers from the kindness box to the class.

Glossary

borrow (BOR-oh)—to use something that belongs to someone else, with permission

interrupt (in-tuh-RUHPT)—to start talking before someone else has finished speaking

manners (MAN-urss)—polite behavior

organize (OR-guh-nize)—to arrange things neatly and in order

patient (PAY-shuhnt)—able to wait quietly without getting angry or upset

polite (puh-LITE)—having good manners; polite people are kind and thoughtful.

respect (ri-SPEKT)—the belief in the quality and worth of others, yourself, and your surroundings

Read More

Nelson, Robin. *Respecting Others.* First Step Nonfiction. Minneapolis: Lerner, 2003.

Raatma, Lucia. *Cooperation.* Character Education. Mankato, Minn.: Bridgestone Books, 2000.

Seder, Isaac. *Responsibility.* Character Education. Austin, Texas: Raintree Steck-Vaughn, 2002.

Internet Sites

FactHound offers a safe, fun way to find Internet sites related to this book. All of the sites on FactHound have been researched by our staff.

Here's how:
1. Visit *www.facthound.com*
2. Type in this special code **0736826467** for age-appropriate sites. Or enter a search word related to this book for a more general search.
3. Click on the **Fetch It** button.

FactHound will fetch the best sites for you!

Index